THE KASHMIRI GIRL

SANDEEP DAHIYA

This is entirely in celebration of youth and its free-wheeling ways.

Contents

Contents

Contents

Contents

Contents

Foreword

Most of these poems were written during the turbulent twenties of my life. In the early twenties, one is pursued by the glorious uncertainties of life. It's a slippery, exciting and critically opinionated path. Don't worry, it's just a surge of extra energy, nothing else. The stage is shaky and realities are yet to get a foothold. You trample a lot of turf like a young colt spraying legs in all directions and galloping just for the sheer causeless fun of it. Of course, there are consequences but they hold their miserable importance in the eyes of the elders only. To the youngsters they are just irritable speed-breakers on the thrilling path.

One's hormonally buzzing self floats in a hazy mist of unripe, raw, juicy, sweet-sour tart of dreams and imaginations striking the moron mass of established norms. The hormonal-storms-fuelled beliefs, views, opinions and dreams create sparks and sometimes thunderstorms. Nothing wrong with that! That's all part of our making. It's a pretty noisy and shaky groundwork born of your 'making' that provides a bit of stability later in life. Ask anyone, most of us are very lenient and forgiving towards our youthful gallops even if these have given us many bruises after the hard falls. We wear them with pride like the symbols of our reaching the peak of the mountain.

Tossed by immaturity and the raw power of youth and age, one hits the extreme ends of emotional scale. It's a massive range of most painful pangs of heart to the ecstatic most reverberations of spirit.

It's a churning of our existence pulled by totally different strings. The product is quite fatty and butter-laced. No wonder, poetry is the handmaiden of the youth. The sediments, the cuts, the corrosion, the erosion, the torrents all unleash a gushing stream of emotions and adventures that swirl past the hard-established conventions and taboos to create a niche for the self.

There is an entire emotional terrain from the bleakest to the brightest as a youthful soul tries to manage the precarious walk on the shaky rope of young age. The same was the case with yours truly. It was a far simpler world in the nineties of the last century and it seems a long time since then. But it's never easy for the youth, be it any age or century. They have their own challenges, agonies, follies and ecstasies.

The sheer shakiness of life in youth propels a multitude of streamlets in one's heart. There is a teasing pull between the head and the heart, wherein the latter most often wins the lots in its favour. The elders may disagree but young people have an entire parallel world, a world that challenges the mundane and boring and firmly etched norms and conventions. We may compromise later in life and settle for a far more contained and restrained life but all of us carry pining nostalgia for our youth because that is when we really challenged the chains that curtail our free flight.

Our follies, which we committed during our youth, still stand better than all the rights of our later years. This is in celebration of youth and its tendency to throw us literally to hit against the ceiling. And the bumps, bruises and little scars that we get along the way never fail to bring a smile on our lips even in the grey years of our old age.

1. The Kashmiri Girl

I read a pastoral poetry,
Among hills, of elysian delight;
Light's incidental rays when
versified moment that,
A little queen burst into view,
Eyes were mesmerized by
that youthful hill girl.
Our eyes met for the first time,
Mine from the plains,
Vehicled, wind-screened, speeding,
And hers from the mountains;
Alluring gaiety of hills and pastures,
One which saw so few;
Forests, snow, pastures, goats,
apple orchards, pines, sheep,
And jovial looks of course at
the vehicles bound for the holy cave.
The other but fed up with
brain-sauced, levelled up intricacies,
And when they butted upon,
Tensioned smiles surfaced,
Some grudges, some complaints,
Fear, excitement and adventure,

THE KASHMIRI GIRL

Mine for the fee-faw going on,
Hers for their sufferings.
Symbolized it two plates,
The Indian and the Eurasian,
Rubbing into each other,
Earthquakes, landslides, killings;
The tale of two religions,
Two geographies also.
She looked coyly,
The deflorating valley hurtled while
a craggy voice around,
Kashmiri girl! Child you were not
to shout for toffee, biscuit from the pilgrims,
Like the small ones doing the same.
A long road the *yatris* travelled,
Mature too you were not,
To snub at the pilgrim's gifts,
From the jovial 14- or 15-stepped podium,
Thou smiled with full brace;
Nature's smile, unchecked and pure!
Made then a V-sign with fingers,
Its meaning you may not even know:
A win for which side?
O floret! Still it was a welcome,
Also a signal to get some gift
from the pilgrims to the holy cave,
Some returning to the plains,

Perhaps never to return again.
Stupefied, I leaned forward,
To accept welcome from the *houri*,
Crowning the celestial beauty around,
Dollishly you smiled again,
Alas, thou were welcoming
a fleeting acardiac tin box,
Sped off which by your side,
Thy fingers somewhat shaking,
Curling to show dejection,
Under your breath
a deflorating smile surfaced,
It was laced with a sweet request,
The excitement in your beautiful eyes
touched peak as the vehicle crossed over,
That emeraldine face blushed,
I was but the poorest man,
Not to possess anything to offer
to that welcoming symbol of love,
Something strung and awakened the self
like the morning song of birds;
The ditty which the heart
just danced to beatific rhythm,
Turned it now the verse
defective at the beginning,
Yes! Fugitive and guilty—
Escaping with the heartless machine,

THE KASHMIRI GIRL

While that velvety cord,
Connected which many Twos,
Was on the verge of snapping,
Moving was I with lolling time;
Chhee, a passive journey
from here to the place called home.
Past it was becoming from the present,
Dirt cheap celerity was taking a toll,
A few seconds ago
the feminine Goddess smiled like full moon,
Chiding *Abba* was now turning it demi-lune,
That soft, juicy, jovial, ripening
bird of love and peace was branched alone.
In that moment of versification
forgot this mortal to symbolize
its ecstasy in any way,
The distance was increasing now
to the farness of hills from the plains,
Like a misbecomed soul,
I convulsed and turned to look back,
And there you shone like a little star,
Bright enough to make time reflow
by the road and your little hamlet nearby,
Crowning the path like
a milestone reached by someone, somewhere,
Missy, thou as rare as a perfect lunar rainbow!
Me lucky to spot one!

I waved at you,
A gesture of defeat, bliss, apologetic and may more,
Good bye perhaps to that
monticule moonet waving back,
Oh, what purity!
Welcoming and forgiving,
Brisking away the netherworld bursting around.
Girl, I looked back till
you turned a faint image
to these eyes,
kept on which hope for the peep-o'-day,
To see the orchid again,
Alas, you but were sheer rarity;
An elusive dreamy appearance,
Which like a fictitious love-tale
painted the heart for a while,
And then you were gone,
For seconds nine or ten
waved when you at the vehicle,
Chiselled in the heart an ogive,
Fade which will not with time,
That small ray emanating
from that montane onyx,
Will always keep travelling
to deep fathoms in my heart.
Tears were of course there,
For that smiling forgiveness,

I gave you nothing,
But the novelette poured
such tomes of wordings in my heart;
That wave of hand,
As rattled on the clatter-hearted pilgrim,
Created big tremors inside,
Enough to break the glaciers
crowning the peaks above,
With suffering peals of thunder inside,
Driven was I forward on the gutted path.
O girl from the mountains!
You smiled for Kashmir whole,
The smile which was part-coloured;
Anguish, fear, communalism, violence
got mixed in an all-pervading whiteness;
That olive branch to a visitor,
Offering the nature's indiscriminating boons around,
Negating all that repressing force
subdues which the free-ways of liberated hearts,
You thus appeared a little saint,
Preaching love, compassion and humanity,
Oneness of nature, humanity and God.
A pilgrim to the valley,
Aching was isolation:
Not of tough clime and testing terrain,
But of hearts rapidly forgetting love,
Kashmir! The crown of India,

The diadem of culture and history,
With man-nature bonhomie,
And cradled heaven on highest terrain,
The seat for spirituality of the great Lord,
And many legends of religion mine,
Meditations in the snowy peaks,
Vales, glaciers, pastures and clouds,
The cheering spectators for truth's delight.
Now the same peaks isolated,
Bombs and bullets yell macabre,
Only suffering cries reach His door,
From these lofty peaks under His chin
guns rattle and bombs create bloody din,
But for whom?
Ishwar or Allah?
Devastated by such a loss,
Hung midair like legendary Trishanku,
Between two extremes,
Trapped in a paradox,
With numbed senses,
Unable to think and feel,
I crossed your roadside hamlet,
And there you were,
Ready to enliven this dazed puppet
with a gold thread having silver core.
That girlish look of eagerness and curiosity,
Excitedly standing on the toes, chin high,

Neck firm like a goddess:
Seemed it a salad-days gyration:
That V-sign,
That smile,
and the wave of hand,
Byeing and good-byeing the visitor,
Hill girl, you stood for the nature around,
Sang a little song of lovely nightingale,
With the scented message that
I am above the things you think,
Waving on the road
you were thus left behind,
Rattled as I along the road,
Knew the authority of 'moving on'—
'Accept not welcome such',
Many uncertainties of the stoppage:
Of Hinduism, Islam and a pilgrim,
Of a Kashmiri Muslim adolescent girl
waving at an Indian Hindu,
And thus helplessly I moved on,
Surrendered to fate and destiny,
Caught in the forces of an orbit,
Mechanised like all the parts
of the vehicle around me,
And then the curve in the orbit
took me out of sight
from that small raylet,

Which was left lost there.
A huge nostalgia piling up already:
Tears in my eyes;
Tears for the curved inevitability,
Tears for a glorious spectacle,
which the fate provided to a stranger;
Fear for the turmoiled smoke
ready to engulf her and her tiny hamlet,
And the Ws about her—
What, when, why, where, whom.
Moisture in the eyes,
Feeling of pain about the damsel,
Who an instant back
poured nature's shower upon me,
And with such an open heart!
With such unselfishness!
A gift for the miser from the plains,
The glorious gift of the hill girl,
From the daughter of clouds,
From the sister of serpentine ravines,
From the playmate of wild breeze,
From the princess of that golden silence.
O bather in the brooks,
Catcher of early sunrays,
O snowy beauty of winters,
Or the flowery one of springs,
I don't know whether

I will see you again or not,
But you will always remind that
nature once stood before me,
versified as a slender hill girl,
looked and waved at me,
That nature once let me read her,
Not the chapter usual
of forest, peaks, snow and brooks,
But a new chapter
in her human version,
Where a sweet swifty angel
chanced across me;
That nature from its abditory
produced a juvenile accretion,
With gaiety, mirth, hilarity;
A page from the Elysium epoch,
With words of unqualified love and smile.
The rugged topography around
saw a goddess in the ripening face,
Those fishy lips moving to fullness,
Those oval eyes acquiring hazel depth,
That nose eager to snatch female coquetry,
Those cheeks eager to be apple-hued,
That forehead proud to recently hear the call of puberty,
That chin with a naughty twitch,
All these depicted the desire and dreams
of the unconquered nature around,

Earlier it lost its smile
in the generality pervading around,
Mother nature, voice whose
came through birds, brooks and sighing mountain winds,
All these and more realized their worth
around your lips,
Whispered as you some sweet word with a smile,
These ears are most unfortunate,
Not to catch that soft whiff,
Which nature tried to voice.
Kashmiri girl!
Mother nature again hid you in its folds,
As suddenly as you appeared,
Lost are you in your small world,
I recollect the sinews now,
Scattered in my soul,
That glimpse sparkled too heavenly,
Melting pains and sparkling ecstasies,
Ever evolving and diversifying,
And me with a birdie hurry
try to relive the same picture again,
Alas, now but I only fail,
Depersonified nature I face now—
Huge mountains, forests, snow
and a large vacant pool of silence,
A wave of pain surfaces from inside,
It goes to the soul's deep well,

And echoes from that cosmic experience
travel far into the distances.

2. The Lone Pine

'Embraced by the pining silence
and stillness of these mute hours,
my detached self grows more independent,
free and aloof like these misty distances
virginally spread out under the moonlight,
The silvery mists kiss my prickly needles
with love free of pride or prejudice.'
Thus mused the lone pine
and felt absolutely fine!

3. The Beauty and the Beast

Greedy, lustful gust of wind
clasped the fragrant petals
of the full-blossomed flower.
Covetous currents of its dark passion
tore the tiny vase of beauty and perfume.
Petals fly with dust in all directions.
The storm doesn't win
and the beauty doesn't lose!
The former loses battle over time and distance
and dies with thorny imprints
left by the stem on its viciously throbbing heart,
The latter spreads its cosily surrendered self
in the limitless folds of peace.

4. The Roguery of Kiss

The sun playing hide and seek among floating clouds,
The humid air wispily whispering a smart secret,
The land lying languidly with overdose of love;
its pining thirst quenched
by the sky's countless kisses and love-drops,
A dove pair mating,
lost in the silent majesty of lusty innocence,
And he holding her hand
with a soft touch to cover stony realities,
A gentle kiss follows
to hide the mutual lies told
to make each other happy and joyful
for the time being.

5. A Paradisiacal Moment

With softly pining majesty,

silence sings a song,

Shadows grow long,

Her soft fingers brace my face

and go along a tear's trace.

Delicate tip of her finger bears the jewel,

A tear,

The tear that would have been

lost as a salty line on my face.

6. Moving on

Lynched by loneliness,
I surrendered to the
sweet tyranny of solitude,
The wounds healed,
The suffering receded,
They moved away
like shifting shadows,
Painful memories lagged behind
and turned milestones on the foggy path,
Of course sweet breeze blows sometimes
and carries syrupy memories from behind,
They leave a smile on my lips
and are again left behind, as I move on,
like sweet path-side flowers,
I look back,
They wave a sweet good bye
with a still sweeter sigh,
And thus we have to move on,
All alone
to our destination next,
And pitch our tent at one fine dusk
and go for a long, long sleep.

7. Love-cuts

Love leaks out of my body,
drop by drop.
Her cuts are incurable:
The non-healing holes;
the ever-existing outlets
for the mellowness inside
to seep out and turn stones.

8. Sugar-coated Hook

Was it your love?
Or the fishing hook of some winning, crushing trait,
On which you had expertly put
smart, suave, attractive and beautiful bait.

9. A Pure Religionist

Religion mine isn't that weak,
So as to cripple me
to condemn and hate some other religion.
I don't have to hate others
to prove love for my own.

10. A Normal Grip

If there is a storm around you,
I mean nasty, leering sea-storm
churned out by the incurable circumstances,
Whining like a dog won't help,
Nor will the majestically brave lion's roar
to tame the storm help you.
It's better that we try to swim
to the best of our humble capacity,
Leave then the rest to the unknown forces.
Believe me,
even the burning core of the nastiest storm,
ultimately embraces
the cool ice block of a genuine effort!

11. Awakening

In the mist-veiled silence of a dream,
I sleep-walked into the crazy grasp
of a thorny bush.
All we just need is a prickly bite
to see the reality!

12. Grand Illusions

With sand-grains grasped in my hands,
fleeting clouds in my heart
and enforced philosophies in my head,
I set out to win the kingdom
that never existed!

13. The Angels of Duality

We hatch our own agonies and ecstasies
in the workshop of our mind,
Deep in a little corner
of our private space.

14. The Runaway Vagabond

In the calm core of my wind-lashed, stormed self,
some unmovable shadow
defines the substance of my being.
I but have been running miles after miles,
chasing mirages to seek my identity.

15. The Journeyman

It doesn't matter
where you come from,
what matters is
where you go;
and more importantly
how you go.

16. A Rain-soaked Moment

Village...

musty...

like a mossy mushroom under a banyan...

rain-lashed...

semi-shaded silvery-haired wise days...

rain-washed greenery greedily sprouting forth...

a love-seeking peacock dancing...

a bee-eater diving for its success

and the dragonfly's failure...

flirtatious swallows riding the airy horses...

a tailorbird throwing loud vocal force

for its 7 gram weight...

a squirrel and a crow fighting for a nut...

a mud-smeared dog losing the force of its barking

against a braying donkey...

paddy standing lugubriously...

and the water sailing above in huge cloudy ships,

ready to melt and shower its love again,

any moment...

17. The Lost Love

A dewdrop slips down
the petal of a full-blossomed rose,
It seems like a tear,
A tear for the black bee that came,
sucked juice and was gone.

18. Shadows under the Light

There is no perfect darkness,
and hardly complete light,
Not entirely good
and perfectly bad either,
Darkness stands because
the light is at some distance,
And light means
the shadows are yet to crawl near,
Here lies the challenge for goodness,
because bad is just a bit away
to unleash itself and dance and sway.

19. The Winter Dawn of My Village

My village under cold, foggy clouds,
Lives, dallies in the wintery days,
The beholder of bare earth and smiling soil
and still closed to the rampaging world,
It's a small corner of dew, mist, frost and all:
Birds, animals, villagers all surrender to the chill,
They too carry icy shades within:
Uninterested and not much conscious of the 'hotty
modernity'.
The dawn taking a yawn after a night frosty,
Like a curvaceous damsel,
after a dreamful, sweet night,
arms stretched to the vigorous pull of youth,
reddish lips in a tantalizing twisted pout,
and breasts firm against any overture uncouth,
Her dreamy eyes shine with maternity universal,
Ready to save this world from the doomed hate,
Her eyes full of love, smiles and dreams.
The westerly breeze sashaying over the budding wheat
like a dusky, nimble-footed beauty,
The soft touch of her heels on the earth—
soothing, assuaging, healing and comforting,

And the wheat spikes open their eyes
to the maternal touch,
Like an infant moves its wispy, sparse eyelashes.
Arrogant crows fly out of the village,
To those dense plantations afar,
With wings cutting the saffron rays,
Cawing labour they will engage in the whole day
and return with the smell of twilight among tired sunrays,
Choosy parrots fly to tastier trees,
Mother nature has extra-pampered them:
The vagrant beauty of colours red and green,
Even nature seems favouring them
more than the blacks,
So they fly in the opposite direction from the crows,
And why not?
Closer they are to nature
than the rookies showing many characters human
in being retentive, querulous and cunning,
So the greens fly higher than the blacks.
Wool-laden toddlers waddle along the streets,
Like little Eskimos,
Their mothers put extra woollen layers on them:
Maternal care swaddled around them,
While they sneak away like tiny explorers
to see a bit more of this world,
Their aged grandparents, their exact analogues
on the other side of the slope,

warm their fragile, old bones around *hookahs* in *chaupals*,
Hollow cheeks buzz with chuckle and logic simple,
Far from the warmth of gushing youthful blood,
They are mere fractions of life,
trying to integrate the group
and form a still-meaningful complete integer,
to live with at least that much of life
that at least would comprise a single, bubbly youth.
The village beauty smiles behind her thin veil:
The moon behind a fluffy curtain of soft clouds,
The sun peering over the cloud's edge,
The star smiling from the farthest distance,--
The sweet enjoyment of ogling at lotus in hazy waters.
The hurried gait to finish her household chores
looking a bit odd on her fine, work-honed curves,
Her tipsy, honeyed ogles,
potent to infatuate the hardest heart,
just fall on crude work,
The locks of hair with style simplest,
The envy of metropolitan beauties of great care,
Worry not o damsel,
The virgin soil of the village
dances around your work-beaten heels;
a chilly breeze kisses your rosy cheeks;
The tiniest particles of the mist cling
to the single lock out of the veil.
And the sun struggles to rise in the east,

Only to look at your shadow moving graciously.
Yes, such is the winter dawn!
Saffron rays cut across the fog,
Gobble up the last traces of the night;
It comes to my village
like a daughter practicing 'nature's care',
right from her birth in every relation.
The rising sun will dry away the dew, mist and frost,
Seedlings straighten up; the burden is off!
Bravo! Every seed off the peasant's hand
fights nature to feed the nation,
Salutes! The farmer's green paint splashed around.
Icy vapours in the village pond
shelter the migrants; many from the Himalayas,
Exiled by the snows,
they live happily, warmly here,
This dawn is proud to host the familiar
crane couple, ducks, pelicans, herons and many more.
Such is my village at dawn,
Ready to go and almost self-sustain,
So few are such places, elsewhere!

20. The Light Beyond

There is light beyond
the deepest dark depth,
There is a bright day
after the ghostly haunts of a nightmarish night,
After a barren famished fight,
there is a full-blossomed spring's delight,
After the pining pangs of separation,
there is a worthy end to the desperation,
After crashing in the gutters,
there is a surge and rise to bathe in holy waters,
After crying convulsions on the lips,
a smile takes honeyed sips,
After the last defeat,
still there is an undying urge to accomplish the feat,
Even when blind with despair,
there is hope hiding and cajoling somewhere,
Even in hate,
love casts its beautiful bait.

21. Love-fangs

I feel the shapeless mass of your love,
It creeps like a venomous reptile
through the garden of my heart,
It furiously hisses,
returning my softest kisses,
I bear the toxic marks
left on my skin by your fangs.
Still I carry your poisonous stones
in the soft cradle of my heart.
Why?
Because I have no choice to hate you,
I can just love you!

22. The Immortal

I know life has rejected me,
And when death will accept me
that time is yet to be!
Till then, O Sufi, is there any light to see?
Yes brother, there is!
It's in being with those
who have been discarded by fate,
Who have laboriously scrawled
and scribbled lifelong
but still have a clean slate;
It's in smiling with innocent dawns;
It's in basking in the sunny charms
of sultry, forlorn lawns;
It's in the faded twinkle of distant stars;
It's in saying goodbye
to the intrigues of one's own internal wars;
It's in being with me,
And the way it is, let it be!

23. A Note from Spring's Deathbed

The spring's traces last,

Hot summers approaching fast,

Languid notes in the air,

A solitary bird's forlorn chirping for musical share,

Drowned in stillness,

this late morning bright and fair,

Sky's dull blue,

Overhanging the earth in paling hue,

But a smaller world is there,

The overall weariness cannot reach where,--

In its self-defined world

in a corner tiny,

The luscious wild flower

still stands brave and shiny.

24. The Smile, the Godliness

O thou wind-lashed flower,
Sadistic nature took rapist bites
at your soft petals,
At each bite and cut it laughed
and licked its blood-smeared lips,
You but stood unfazed for
beauty and fragrance.
The storm meanwhile
kept on increasing its fury,
But for how long?
It ran out of its fuel,
And stood panting and drained out,
When the night and the storm died
and a beautiful, warm, sunny day was born,
the profound flower stood majestically resplendent!
Its storm-lashed petals
more beautiful than ever!
Why?
Because never did it let
the smile go off its face!

25. The Flower's Tears

Flowers aren't supposed to weep,
Even if their petals are vandalized,
As the raping storms
spit all their fury
on their fragrant face.
It's just for beauty's sake, they say,
And tears on its petals are no tears,
These are unholy signs of its revolt.
So they just expect it to smile
while their poisonous fingers
greedily tear away petal after petal.
Listen you merciless fools!
A flower bears the pain most!
Even though its unfading smile
never allows it to surface on
its smiling face.
But a flower weeps unseen in the
dark hours of the night,
Humans, the dew-laden petals that you
gratify your senses with
are in fact the tears of that
soft petalous self.

26. The Mother

I'm the fire,
Who can fathom my
burning core's plight?
They dance in my warmth
and see only the light!

27. The Bleeding Flower

Flower you were always beautiful!
Those balmy days blossomed your wonderful petals.
Then the weather changed,
Stormy winds, furious storms
took sadistic bites at your soft petals.
Bleeding flower,
You but kept your smile,
Nature's fury lashed you,
Biting winds lynched you,
Like a sinful rapist they groped you,
You but smiled forgivingly.
Now the sinner stands
robbed of its fury,
And you smile more beautiful than ever.
Love, beauty and harmony prevail,
Hate, anger and lust always fail.

28. A Moment's Pining Call

Staring at the misty past
and forcing myself not to see
the future eager to unfold itself too fast,
I wave at the nostalgic strains
still beckoning and alive,
How I wish I could dive
back into the pools of the past,
To have my moments last
at a place that held me in its cradle soft,
That soulful embrace which still holds me aloft!

29. The Last Prayer

It has been months since
I last lit my faith's lamp,
So many days have passed since
prayers chimed in my dark den's air damp,
My meditating self,
Now gives atheistic yelp.
Lost my faith!
Lost my prayer!
Lost my rituals!
Lost my meditative trance!

30. The Coin

My story is strange,
To understand it, you need less brains
and more open of a heart,
I was a coin with lots of shine,
Then I passed through hundreds of hands
one after the other,--
The moulding darkness gave me fearful creep,
And I was lying at the top of the mint's heap,
Somehow I was given to a young guy,
Who tossed me in air and made me fly,
Then I was given to an old lady,
She kept in a place that was very shady,
I noticed I had lost my shine,
And I didn't look young and fine.
That is because I had grown old,
Now, I know my life's story is told,
There are endless scars
and imprints on my soul.
I have lost my value in my own esteem,
But they still haggle over me sometime.

31. Oh God, that Hollowness!

Oof that soul entombed in misery!
The ragamuffin, the beggar,
Great potter's potsherd he was,
Those decaying, yellow teeth
splashed and sprayed this world
with misery and incurable jaundice.
His trifle weight could outweigh
the fattest people in the street,
And eyes ever so colourless
could gobble down springs all.
The ears like the deepest gorges,
could accommodate a billion sympathies
and countless words soft,
The tongue would talk to millions,
if the opportunity arose,
Alas, the milling humanity around
pretended not to be visible at all,
People scampered past with the
careful eyes of a cautious thief;--
saving both their conscience and money.
His emotions lay buried deep
in his famished breast,

This was his treasure trove,
He kept it safe,
Afraid to take them out,
lest they slaughter these as well,
His bleeding heart would have
painted this planet in gloomy red.
A dog, cat poop, wrappers, dust, snoot, phlegm,
And he just another addition to these,
Almost indiscernible in his insect kingdom,--
Dusting, rottening, petty and cast-out.
The accusing emptiness,
And the hallowed universe around,
Holding his mocking lighthouse,
Throwing feeble, exposing light over the
fallacies lolloping under the abounding waves
of the booming sea of hilarity and well-being.

32. The Feminizing Man

Fragrance scented and colours prismatic,
Flowers seduce with surrendering softness
and intoxicating aesthetics,
This alluring, sweet poison slays many,
Parasitically it creeps into
the hibernating, sleepy male vitality,
And the red, gushing blood of sense and sanity
turns into silly swirls of bluish oblivion.
Foolish torrents of bewitching beauty follow,--
A marvellous decolourisation of
flesh, vision and potency!
The woman does the same with the man,--
Her moves lie under the surface,
Letting loose amorous tremors,
The tamed beast clinging to feeble, unmanly chains:
the emotions, cooings and the mellowed stone,
Then she slaughters the prey most manly,
Bravo! Salutes to the femininity:
the hardest heart under the shield softest.
Weakness has its strength in vulnerability,
Don't mistake power by the steel in muscles,
Soft flowers and seductive women
thrive on the dew shower of temptations,

Eyes thirsty, pining senses;--
The altars of the insected, infatuated masculinity,
More the offerings on the altar,
more the Goddess thrives,
So many wither to bloom a smile
in her sly eyes.
But her demands from the worshipper
are never satiated,--
Greedy Goddess!
She thus hunts around,
But greed can never make one complete,
So she just remains a fraction,
Men cut themselves to the same
to complete her missing portion,
The happy Goddess then
laughs at the follies of the maimed.
Black bee, man sacrifice to
prove the worth of an ounce of femininity,
Rivers eat mountains, while the stones
surrender to the fluidity of the majestic masseur,
The woman meanders to fragment the man,
Making round, harmless, cuddly pebbles.
As the feminine dreams web around,
The ensnared caterpillar hums the songs of love,
The spider salivates and chuckles,
The trap of seduction,
The cobwebs of death,

The river thus triumphantly
rolls on with mighty boulders,
The song of macabre swirling
among the torrential giggle and frightening moan.
Femininity wins through its weakness,
The flowers smile and bloom on showers of tears,
The woman makes the man a means to her end,
Travels on his strong back
to reach her destination
and find the purpose of her life.

33. A Brief Love-grip

Love loops around on an early winter day,
In the heart, endless things to say,
Shines a gently warm, bright ray,
Before the icy winters shout, and chuck it all out,
Enjoy and make hay!

34. The Whisper

The mighty lord whispers in a soft voice,
'My son grow thou strong
and sire chances for those without any choice!'

35. Sweet Enemy

Though your enemy, I am sweet!
My neck thus deserves a softer treat!

36. My Mind, My Buddy

Be the seat of my strength, not weakness.

Be the seat of kindness, not cruelty.

Be the source of light, not darkness.

Be the source of energy, not idleness.

Be the source of creativity, not limited vision.

Be the source of love, not hate.

Be the source of smiles, not tears.

Be the source of happiness, not suffering.

Be the seat of optimism, not pessimism.

Be the seat of gain, not loss.

Be the source of help, not obstruction.

Be the seat of leadership, not just sleepwalk.

Be the seat of a better human being.

Be the source of a more loving person.

O my mind, my seat of potential,

take my journey further.

Choose the better half of all the dualities for me.

One should keep reminding one's mind.

Repeatedly.

Daily.

With eyes closed with a fervent request.

It's a very nice, nutritious pre-breakfast food.

37. The Voice Inside

Forget about the hoot and holler
emanating from the world outside,
And give an ear to the soft and murmurous
cooings emanating from the soul,
It has a soft and sympathetic
message for you only,--
your most personal message,
meant only for you,
Listen to these delicate chimes,
It'll help you in finding peace in chaos,
In getting a foothold in the stampede,
In feeling rest, repose and respite
amidst constant buffeting by the world around,
It'll help you in breaking
the hardest of superficial layers,
which suffocate and limit your identity,
And put you face to face with
your true self, your real worth,
Listen to it, close your eyes,
And pay attention with all your heart,
Just for a change,
don't look far, look closest at yourself,
It'll be as uneventful as looking

at a dust particle around your feet,
But it changes the universe for you,
You will have the biggest message
in the softest of whispering phrases!
And it'll help you in finding yourself.

38. Jewelled Vagary by Nature and Man

White-pearled necklace smiles,
Of cobweb, with dew beading it,
Silvery, on a bonsai-like acacia,
In murky morning, fog and cold.
Prickly branches sprout, frozen,
Empty-headed, standing still and mute,
Like a bribed beauty silent;
Jewelled throats disclose nothing.
The fog-vaulted sky above,
Vapours riding nuclei unseen,
Making things around appear as sprites,
And the necklace among the bones and thorns.
Gallowed! Thus serene forever,
Like the ever-impressed eyes portrayed,
Follow which the observer always,
Greedy to be jewelled more.
Nature's goldsmithy and the man's:
The necklace in the thorns,
The other making the skin prized more,
Beauty thus defined, thrives on donated bounties.

39. Drawing, Sketching Webs of History

People come and go,
with genealogies spinning history,
Everything changes to survive,
Similarly, man becomes his opposite more.
Fast riding jockey he is,
Sticks to the saddle of time,
His horse trampling the turf,
And the cheers eating the dust around;
The 'eagle's eye' spotting the winner
among the beasts riding the same,
Gallops match the applauds around
to cut the finishing line first.
Whoever may be the lucky one,
It's nothing but simply
a line drawn over the last one,
And many parallels following.
What did the winner get?
Nothing but the smallest
glimpse of others doing the same;
Irony drips from the dusted moments,
Look, the victor ponders back the maximum,
Trickles which to zero

for the last one cutting across.
A trophy, a V-sign, a horse's smile,
That is what they give him,
And some rest on the podium;
That is what life is,
Dropping every skill of ours
on the back of a beast
to carry us as a victor,
Half-man, half-beast,
we leave nothing but litter around;
Exhausted and throbbing hearts.
So much of the course is
trampled to death,
only for the thinnest line
connected by similar tangential lines;
With milestones of eulogy,
And battlefields in between,
This is what we call
history, progress and more.

40. Death in a Forest

Night was falling in the jungle,
With stars smiling from a cold sky,
Early mist making a drink
to inebriate the trees through the night,
And the leaves preparing for a dewy bath.
A dark man matching the night's colours,
Stumbled across the decaying windfalls,
His skin clad in more darkness,
White teeth flashed to life,
Like water in the abyss of a well,
A sigh of agony poured out
warmth in the imposing cold.
All vestiges fading out of sight,
Yet, two gentle eyes like an elephant's said,
'Live and let live';
His burning self gave
some warm solace to the dewy, cold leaves,
His bright foot-soles drummed
on the decaying leaves,
Sowed seeds of life among death and decay.
The music approaching the forest's centre,
With stars applauding
and the trees swaying to the tune,

Nature styled his hair:
Curls, locks, dust matched the jungle's disarray,
He stumbles now more
and finally sits under a tree,
Sleeps then to eternity,
The last trace of life mixed
with the darkness around;
The morning came to enliven everything,
but not the last trace of night.

41. Escapades from the Pyre

Hot ash of the cremated,
There lies the voice of the Himalayas,
Stood which rock firm,
Now turned into grains few
by the holy flames,
Fire ate the fire—
an elaborate oasis
combusted to a desert small.
Hot air rising upwards
with liberating soul
and mourners' tears,
To make rain of it,
which will shower upon a flower
manured by the cemetery's ashes;
'Will' dies never,
The passion of a life whole
now forms the flower of a single day!

42. Jailed by Destiny

With every sinew losing out,
There lies the nest of my hopes,
Scattered like dying, gasping fishes,
Destiny chuckles over the vaporizing,
fading signs of its opposition.
Why not? Sinners are those
who toil against the lines of fate
drawn on our palms;
The web of destiny
that limits and chains ventures all,
And the puppets merely dancing to its tune.
Every pulse, dying or born,
Here in this world, or the other;
From the first cry to the last in an abyss,
We are just tools in the great reaper's hands,
The cruel General leads an army
comprising we the puny foot-soldiers,
Fighting against each other;
Instruments and weapons in millions of hands,
The leader uses one to cut, thrash and mow the other.
Each hope and cause great
turn the sins bigger for the mighty ringleader,
And I am the biggest sinner,

With my misplaced ideals and misfitted compassion;
Now I stand amidst my garbage,
Unworthy, hopeless and thoroughly beaten.

43. To Talk Small; To Talk to Earth

Hiccups come whooshing like arrows,

Bowed backs, tension-stringed souls,

The tension stored from the time immemorial,

And the sobs go squelching.

Ye squeak only, bad marksmen!

Your shots just firecrackers

around the towers of the exploiters,

The towers hanging sprucely, with talons.

Tag-rags! Thou from yore,

From womb to the grave,

Cry just one by one;

Individually and separately,

Pouring saline anguish on wasted cheeks.

Ever eager to attack

the heavenly vaults for the evils all;

Hands ready to break His head,

Never but the real cause lying nearest.

You murder prophets easily,

Never but support the champion of liberty,

So you remain as ever,

Ugh, historically the same beaten class!

Yoke fellows! Please let Him rest,

If eager to weep yet,
Then cry ghoulishly in a chorus,
Like Shiva's drumbeats.
Or waste not anguish in tears,
And noises that fall on ears deaf,
Shout Tally Ho! For history's sake,
Let it progress by a different type of change.

44. Fenced Jaunties

Billions jangle, survive, obey
the instructions of a single urge;
Of infinity,
finites which itself
by kraaling simpletons in a common craze,
It lounges to exist forever,
And the night-walkers sleep-walking,
Moving in the shadows
and believing it to be a bright sunny day.
The ever prudent God, the shrewd muleteer!
Measures His fathomless depths
with puppets playing on strings of ecstasy and tragedy;
The luminary lights a bit of the stage,
Death and darkness but circle around,
where the light of reason and faith
escapes with the escaping soul.
The five senses slipping over the oily scalp;
Tongues turned steely by quoting borrowed words,
Nostrils get clogged with the smell of decay,
Eyes take the last shot of the puzzles around,
Ears drum for the last to the eternity's beat,
The touch of mystery leaves more clueless,
And all it turns out is a

journey from nowhere to nowhere.
Sheep peeping across the fences barbed,
Hoy! Bleating jargon longing to voice the truth last;
The final mystery meanwhile
buried underwater like the lotus roots,
Above, a water lily blooms under the owl light,
Excitedly flickering to pamper
the Himalayan vanities scattered around.

45. Beloved, Thou art Life's Sestet

Your love became soul's food,
O my lyrical lyre special;
Intoxicated was every pore and cell,
Mind lost its relevance,
Only heart ruled over the show.
Body vibrated with thy name,
Love-blinded, the eyes saw only your dreams,
Thy voice drummed on the plane of my being,
Millions of nerves sensed only you.
Time and this world sped off for me,
I got time-frozen for the eyes deep and brown;
Red, curvy lips eager for a smile,
That moony face bewitched me.
Path's prickles smiled like you,
I stepped over, where was the pain!
The mind didn't reason with heart anymore,
Even in sadness I glowed with visions thine.
Now, away you are; ever to be seen?
The soul cries, lynches each second passing by,
But, thou are my last lines,
And will remain so, till I die.

46. An Atom Leaps, Snakes Hiss Around

Purple clouds, fires ablaze,

The atom danced profusely,

The soil around its feet got burnt,

The choreographer talked peace in future,

Peace! In invisible poisoned wombs,

Not in the beak of the pigeon white,

The reactor fumes coloured it black,

The black messenger flew around for fifty years,

Talking of peace with its

tearing talons ready to prey upon

anyone who won't believe in manufactured peace.

Death centred on missiles privileged

blackened earth dark without peace,

A trauma of half century,

When thousand Buddhas smiled and feigned peace,

A peaceful country now becomes

more so with another noise underground,

And lo an earthquake endangers all

who had been made too safe by

the numerous stockpiles around;

The nuclear snakes,

which can bite for once and all,

Point now poison in an earthworm,
Why not? A few furrows by the latter
lay bare the hollowness beneath.
The nation that never hissed,
Only jumped like a rabbit under attack,
Now takes shelter in the steely womb,
which the python cannot digest,
Nor can play the cat and mouse;
And the mighty keepers of peace
go making floods of tears around.

47. Destinies in Drunken Laps

Like a drunken old man,
The tree sways to the December breeze,
Intoxication of age, alcohol in one,
The other with the spirit of the air,
A boozy synchronism!
The old man and the tree,
Winy hearts and the swings.
Legs unsteady; walked too much,
The tree too, does it
sillily in the syrupy cold,
Veins and vegetations drunk!
Synchronicity involves two more elements:
A caterpillar among the leaves,
Clutching like the grandson
in the grandpa's fragile, shaky arms,
And so the swaying moments go on,
The tree and the old man gyrate,
The infant, the caterpillar hold.
Really gentle is the breeze,
Makes not noise among the leaves,
Soufflés inside the body old,
Gentle and feeble same,

Very calm and noiseless!
Some leaves now and then
break off and fall serenely;
A sylvan goddess plucking them,
Similarly, the likes of the old man,
Full with age, go heavenwards,
The leaves around the caterpillar's,
The old men around the boy's,
Calmly fall one by one,
But they hold on,
The caterpillar and the child.

48. Firefly, Thou art Life's Sparkle

Firefly, you are nature's cutest sparkle,
Twinkling to celebrate the mysterious wedding,
And dance to the tune of crickets and katydids,
Thy single leap in the air
matches ours from the caves to Edison.
Glow the branches like a Christmas tree;
Swirl over lake muddy like a lighthouse;
Caged in the puffs of hair, thou smile,
Starry beetle, thou cast a dim light
on an eulogy unknown
on a grave remote in the forest.
The wind whirls around you,
But you still glow like a candle
fighting for life by the deathbed,
Glow thou in the haze of winters,
Like the auroras of the Poles.
On the tender palm of a child,
Thou glow still to light the future
printed on the rosy, soft skin,
Thou have passed many hands,
And read the lines of
Hitlers, Gandhis and many more.

Sparkle like a gem from
the poorest of a thatched hut,
Make them the Kings of the world,
Shikara, cross, dome and *stupa*,
You sit on all of them
and still retain your real self.
From the moments of ecstasy supreme
to the predator's clutch,
thou only smile,
To light and glow,
Touches which a lonely heart
to make it alive and hope again.

49. Beyond Moon and up to the Soul

The lonely star twinkles for me,

Shining still brighter than the full moon,

Full hearted in the cold, milky sky,

While others sleep to the moon's lullaby.

It casts pointed, long shafts of arrows,

Over chilly, rounded, moonlit landscape,

Engraving rays play filigree

with the ghosts loathing light, but out now!

Meanwhile, ogles this world just the beauty 'round';

Encircling lewd stupidity,

Destined to beat the same path,

The same journey and its similar vanity.

I welcome the winks from the

fluctuating one, whose needly rays venture into

the deepest corners of the heart;

Ditches, ravines unfortunate,

where the round beauty's shower reaches never,

So they also smile as fairy rings,

Like prosperous moonlit palaces;

Caper and pearl in abalone come to life,

As its pointed rays caress the prickles

and seep through the entrance narrow.

Needle away the fear in a nest,

As parents return not and the nestlings huddle;

Peep through the thatched roof,

Help the feeble lamp inside,

Battle then the corners dark;

Streak into the narrowest gorges in minds,

where luxurious moony rays reach never,

Star, thou light up

far more than we ever believe.

50. At What Cost, O Thou City?

Lost world or call them worlds,
On the pavements, by flyovers,
In slums, by traffic lights,
On railway stations, and bus stands;
A trail ablaze,
Howling, hissing in its smouldering stupor.
Serpentine curves of life amidst
roads glutted with tired travellers
and buildings choked with bleak elegance;
Each bend thrusts a shock wave,
Badged with the numbers of struggle
people falter, bawl, hackle and sneer
with thick-veined throats and emptying souls.
The urban rosary and its beads:
The halt imposed by a red light,
A mother in torn, soiled clothes,
He/she held in arms and rags,
Pleading in front of the windscreens,
And the wealthy rag-picker
searching lust in the garbage;
Green light beckons the stampede once again,
And taking a carnal sip for free

the already privileged reveller jolts away.
Beggars feigning sleep among foot taps;
Humanity dancing to the tunes of hard heels,
Wheels rumble overhead,
As the trams screech and cringe over the bridge,
Killing by sparing them to live in a mass grave.
A big car chirrs and whirrs
and smiles glossily to defracture the void,
The puffiness hovering around the wheel,
Alas, spacious more for
accommodating the emptiness of the soul;
Rich eulogies for the poor graves around.
Lost worlds piled up in a bigger one,
Fed on something squeezed tight and narrow;
Ghostly and visible not,
Its spirits turned wooden,
And multiplying at mere pin-drops,
What to talk of human efforts, Metro?

51. The Winter Sunset in our Fields

The night is taking birth,
Sunset is imminent thus,
Over the fields cropped,
And silvery mist upcoming,
With the silent majesty of
the sunbeams gently smiling still.
The day, like a minimalist,
Looks sunward to get
yellowish orange traces last,
The sundown moment!
Mingling day and night,
With the sunbeams garlanding,
Which one? Day or night?
Guava, blackberry, mango,
Wild not, but tamed in the orchards,
Stand silent and still,
Their natural character somewhat lost,
Which they laugh away
for some purpose human,
They with the brethren wild
along the canal embankments,
Stand as spectators for the great handover.

Wheat saplings turned plantlets now;
Few inches tall and strong,
To go into the dark
without crying; no fear.
The cawing of a raven,
And a parrot's cherishing tone,
All speak of a day gone,
Distant howl of an owl
from a lone banyan big,
Sounds like a factory hooter,
To awaken the ploughman
from his submission to the work hard,
And realize the world beyond the field.
The long-shadowed sun picture:
A weaver bird's nest
hanging still and safe,
Similarly, the mushroom huts
warm with the lights glowing now,
All seem ready to face
the upcoming dark for the day next.
A cuckoo sings
a little song of bravery
for the hut, the nest
and everything at the dark front.
A crow ogles at the subsiding
redness in the south-west,
Whose vanishing traces

leave its eyes parted wide
and smirking with amazement,
Suddenly, realizing the need of time,
Off it goes with a flutter.
This slow acceleration of
the day into the night;
The gentle fluidity of the light and the dark
embracing and melting into each other,
The gentlest of a brace,
The slow pace,
Unnoticeable bonhomie,
And biggest will be the change;
The change as snaily
as some minutest growth to the wheat saplings.
Thus the sunset is imminent,
Moments stand calm and meditative;
Like we at the birth time
know nothing of the life ahead.
The cool air and the mist
with their dense brush,
Paint a picture tranquil,
With the protagonists standing still,
Save some small movement
among the boyish wheatlings,
And the 'painted lady' butterflying.
The sun goes down further,
Its rays now dissolve

in a woodpecker's eyes
perched atop a tall eucalyptus;
Undefined colour of the painter's disk,
Thus, the sunset is imminent;
The scarecrow in a field,
The proxy owner in the farmer's absence,
Begins now to enliven,
With each degree of the sundown,
It enlivens more and more
to protect the child crop;
The farmer's self symbolized through
the effigy turned human,
Or ghostly, in the dark.
The rim goes below,
Thus it's all over for the day!
The sadness of the moment,
Or the joy of the job done,
And they all stand sunless,
In a state of sweet sorrow
for the celestial minstrel gone,
But still the moment is
pleasing for the soul.
Although everything
may not glow like a diamond,
But like an ill-formed sapphire,
It has its maze,
Where everything has got

mixed feelings, mixed appearances.

52. Believer, Atheist or Agnostic! Which Path?

Religion is made a spade

in the hands which hypnotize

the masses blindfolded, hoping for cures;

Remedies for why, what, when…

The religionist!

The crowd before the sermonizing hands,

The lucky ones looking for

good fate's another instalment,

And the majority begging their first,

Denied to them till now.

Awe-struck!

Stupefied thus, they squat,

The mighty grip around the tool's handle

meanwhile rakes up further ritualistic earth,--

The great spadework!

By the hands preaching, hypnotizing the audience,

who cannot see beyond the fence,

Get up when they after the show,

See apostles build up,

answering meaninglessly

the great queries of what, when, why, how…

And more lines get written to theology,

The magic book of all panaceas.
The Pandora box!
Opens with uncountable spectacles,
And the tears of agony, joy, everything,
The chorus now grows further,
Politicians, bureaucrats, corporate…
The expertise! The hypnotizers join
with their ever-elusive *tete-a-tete*;
Spreads His gospel theatrically,
And the mass stupefaction multiplies.
The great religious band!
A pair of hands symbolizing God's,
Music in the background by the experts,
And the hypnotized cloud enlarges
from the religious opera house,
Reaches the lone hut, villages,
states, countries and continents,
And finally the farthest universe,
Enlarges it too much,
To infinity!
The hypnotized universe!
Ever multiplying talks about why, what, when…
Stamps from the Pandora box:
Devotional, devout, pious, religious,
After the show, they all come out,
Stamped foreheads, the believers!
Beguiled by the tricks of the gloved hands,

If hypnotized not still,
They bark at him 'Atheist',
The one who questions what, when, why…
This unstamped, unorthodox outcaste,
Counters the divine oratory
with sizzling counter-points,
Questions upon answers to what, when, why…
And they neigh in desperation.
Opens the atheist now
the Pandora box of his own,
The box with tricks to
to undo all the great work done,
Another magic book!
But for the negative infinity
by a 'single god' over all the godheads,
To dehypnotize the public,
Too great an effort!
But still a small whiff,
Unable to create a storm
of negative winds,
and negative why, what, when…
Devotional winds blow around, meanwhile,
So what do we have now?
The majority hypnotized, blindfolded,
And someone in tantrums,
Arguing testily and
striking as many heads as possible,

To awaken them from the slumber,
Alas! He but is negative more, restless more.
What do we have now?
A dish with spice:
Orthodoxy spiced with unorthodoxy,
Hence tasty, juicy more.
Someone is also sitting somewhere,
His existence too earthly,
The real dweller of the earth!
The agnostic!
Questions or their counters
don't reach this self-religioner,
So, worry not about what, when, why…
Beyond the confines of luck and destiny,
This conscious, relinquishing soul
has outflown too much from inside,
Vacuum thus created, where
cravings die and magic tricks fail.

53. Reaching Heavens with Wings

There I zoom like a bird,
Imagination matching its flight,
Aerial view of the panorama below,
With earth laughing, cajoling,
But, I sense the futility of its smile,
Which myriads personify by
living, sweating in the furrows.
Bird's eye! Yes, I just see
the scenery general most,
Without 'particularity' any,
Strikes which at the chance first,
No, I don't create particularity,
Not of woman and things tempting,
My 'bird's eye' slipping over the edges,
Making curves of generality,
So universal is my love,
Not to be caught by a single heart.
O man, fly like a bird,
With wings carrying across
the infinity of the universe;
Never become stones of personality,
Bound by specialities many,

Whom many things strike
like bugs eating the dead;
When every incident and trend
lynch the prisoner chained.
So fluff away like a bird,
At the trivial most instance to save life;
I do the same like a bird,
Shy away from everything,
And fly away, tail twitching,
To the horizons where nothing pinches;
No love, hate or nymph-like thing
cling to the mind to create trauma,
Yes, I wish to be only such!

54. Our Existence Torched: The Life

Life is like a shooting meteor;
Just a whizzing-past star,
Whose starting point nobody sees,
But of course, visibility of the end,
Wow! Abruptness with a vengeance,
And wormy annihilation in
capacious, unbound space.
We are the shots from the unknown;
Intentional or accidental?
Predetermined or chancy?
Willy-nilly, we just roll over
the calamitous mud of the slippery path.
Life sparkling with a fizz,
Pain, joy, smiles, weepings and ecstasies
swoop like a meteoric trail in the sky;
Born to soil the earth,
Like the broken star's residue,
We add to the primal matter.
From unknown to the unknown,
We are known as a 'life',
Just as the luminosity of
a shooting, breaking star.

55. The Old Man and the Hut

The old man and the hut,
Reed and grass sheltered
like the old bones in his body frail,
And both of them hold
on the brink of life and death,
being and non-being,
Wispy fleecy in a hush,
Penned down by the destiny when
she was on flying clouds
and wanderlust.
The old man, nobody knows
from where he came,
Stranger even than a foreigner;
Wind-fallen in his own land,
A pedigree, on the verge of
ending on his side;
Nobody to inherit the wishy-washy shelter.
Nature habituated to them,
The old man and the hut,
A small brook, a forest averagely thick,
And a loneliness persisting,
Save a sortie or two

by an occasional adventurer,
Who may come to spread the self.
Nothing changes here,
Except time through his wrinkles
and some sinew blown from the hut,
A marvellous, fluid constancy of nature:
Same chirps of the birds,
Same bubbling in the brook;
Also the same generality,
Except one particularity,
The old man and the hut.
Wintery shivers in his humble bed,
With eyes staring at the roof,
Giving strength to it
against the raindrops naughty,
Longing to play with him.
In summers, he sleeps outside,
In the open, under the starlight,
Too much light above!
But alas, too far!
Spread out thus in the open,
A look into the stars above
with the eager eyes of a child,
Then close with a peep
into the depths of age,
Thus sleep layers over him,
He knows not when,

And where, nobody cares.

56. Sympathy Game

Disability, permanent or short-lived,

Is a cause of distress extreme,

For, sulks one in the ripped self,

A mere breaking star among shiny thousands.

Satisfaction of the competition

being the fuel of life,

As nothing else is society

but relentless rivalry among the capable.

Abhorred is robust and fit here,

Know they, fitness is nothing

but a hindrance in their path,

And cursing goes everyone.

No time for the interests common,

As heart has shrunk much,

Bellicose is man, bellows only;

Bereaved human is rival such.

Ah! The redeeming glimmer exists,

Thank God! Thrown is someone

out of the race mad; abed is faculty,

Sprouts then the sympathy fountain.

Emotions, adages pour out

for the poor player out of the race,

Admire they the infirmity in him,

Already dead he is without playmanship.
It's the disease and disability,
Making you suffer lot,
Yet smile at it,
For it has aroused an emotion precious.

57. When I was Small

Bird was I, flew tirelessly
in what was to become golden past,
And the innocent, humane most,
Matured are the wings now,
But lost is 'big' in its bigness.
World was then,
as small as me, and beautiful;
Distorted are both today,
As I trample the 'soft me',
And the world grows up harsh.
Things only trivial now,
Hugely inspired that delicate heart,
The urge today being fat;
Lost is imagination and heart shrunk,
Mind has become iron clod almost.
Weak was then I,
for flying too high and far,
I flap wings too much today,
But tired I am,
as wings fall short of the desires.
Then I had only heart,
Too big and I lived,
I only survive today

with a tiny heart;
Vast is my mind today.
Frightened was I then of
most common, simple things,
But now, bold I am,
not to fear any inhumanity,
Present of that past, I am.

58. Heaven under the Hot Sun

The sun marches north; sultry evenings,
Bulging wheat pods await rituals last,
The wizened golden stalks ready
to surrender the fecundity crowning them;
Farmers cut, gather, reap and mow
with bull's eye and parental care,
Birds filch every lost grain in the soil,
Crops smile daughterly in the days bright,
Hats off! Accept they the rites last with smiles.
A dog, dry-mouthed, awaits master's lunch,
Birds, their beaks full, ferry the cargo to the nests,
A bunny runs in the fields bare,
looks for some hideout any;
Above, a gibberish crow caws a laugh,
A sparrow looks into a waterhole,
Few drops there and a hornet gnarls over,
A child plays under a tree's hot shadow,
The air dances around the working mother;
Plays with pollen in hair long,
And she doing filigree with grains,
The locks of her hair try to protect
the 'moon' shining in the glaring day,

She jerks them away and smiles.

59. Thrives my Village

Life and people stroll easily,
Fast and furious urbanity outside
being the sole kicker at the easy pace,
It's a rickety creaking pace,
Measuring minutes in hours,
Hours in days,
It retains its creaky pace
even if the land share may shorten,
or enforcing come the modernity's grip.
They are all here,
and the same poor villagers,
Nature's cruel bite or the soft hand,
It's all but life whole;
Be the dripping roofs,
Mud in the streets,
Or 'life drops' in the fields,
All are the basics here.
The children too simple
and the creations of adaptations,
Stuffed in the studies captive
wait they for the last bell,
God's pity or else,
Weak and empty they are not,

and will survive through life all.
The elders amazed at the change,
Try to catch up with the new,
But survive they only,
Age is a curse,
for it deprives one of the productivity,
Outcaste they are;
assemble and remain in a unified maze.
Simplest is the society here,--
The psyche prone to ignore,
The hands eager to work more,
And hence the life going with easy lore.

60. Footsteps Lost

Walking I was, some day,
Along a track; a tracery it was
of those who passed in the past;
'Hurried only they,' I mused; left poor trail,
Mingled which easily in the earth.
The beaten dust beneath looked
easy for a venture fresh,
Swayed I with pomp and pride,
for easy was the poor path to tread;
And admiring all, went I with a happy song.
The soil below seemed
only poorly tottered in the past,
As no footprint was distinct,
I will leave a permanent one,
Thought I, proud of youth and time.
Praised I everything,
Fresh and exuberant all,
Trying I was, to put
steps distinct, firm most,
So that mingle they not in dust soon.
Alas! Pinched the sun bitterly,
Shrewd wind howled; Hated I all,
Lost rhythm and balance, and tottered,

Vanished my footprints right there,
Sadly sighed I for their short span.

61. Live Bright in Dark

Dream it was, happened
between conscious and unconscious,
Lost I was in gloom, but
made it the flaccid self alive,
Passing was the night and
lying I was, stretched piteously.
Weak to the extreme;
Lined horizontal I was and dormant,
Existed so low, puny and dwarf,
But raised it me, telling
so little was left of the night;
Awake! Compensate the scrawny past,
I now realised, obscured was I by
my own fears in the darkness of night,
So low I'd made myself,
And piteously near to the ground.
Certainly some were there,
Who valiantly fought the gloom,
And were alive among the dead,
Realised I, lived they more,
Enjoyed the panorama swathed in darkness,
Made they full use of the pitch dark,
While the rest slept among the dog's bark.

Vertical I turned myself,
Decided to be among the few,
Little was left of the night,
And lived then brightly,
With that great dream
shining in my eyes.

62. Friendship Unsocial

A lot of relations throng,
God creates some,
Draw we some in the social garb,
But nothing relates humans,
as does friendship divine.
Lynched by formality is this world,
For nothing is society but rules of convenience;
The individuals form society by
becoming ceremonious, social to all,
Doctrined are thus the relations here.
But, friendship evades laws,
Most informal as it is,
Sheds away all cautioned, decorated self;
Enlarges the individual's scope with soul freed,
Suffocated who earlier with the chained self.
All behave stilted, skewed here,
Some for their own greed,
Also, some for others' harm,
Thus framed in cunningness becomes each,
As nothing else is society.
But friends share all,
Break they walls of social norms and etiquette,
Multiplies individuality to

become a spacious whole,
Ethereal is this 'unsocial' supplement.
Many envy the enhanced persona;
Individuality lost among the friends,
But, the enlarged self never
goes astray; such is
friendship, fracturing formal rules.

63. Humane is My Village

The air is laden with cooperation,
No thorny apathy;
No mob to throng the cornered self,
And murderous individualism axing hearts,
Here, we have a mixed self: the kind behemoth.
Neither bucolic love and unity whole,
Nor nucleated as in concrete jungles;
Limited is the spectrum; holds which
tender human bond still strong, and
live we all in slow majesty of decent unconcern.
The hunger and thirst for electricity and water,
Though dents the moral fabric a bit,
But in patience and forbearance the real self prides—
To bear all hardships and deprivations;
And adapt to disadvantages all.
The people still carry habits, conventions old,
Burdened further by the stuff new,
Still, carry they the rusted self with rural pomp,
Habituated to ignore and move on,
Veneers which as rough pride of the ruralites.
The commuters to the city carry old bags,
Hoping to fetch something new,
The very same villagers still they are

whose rough-hewn character
breathes with unease in the city big.
Still able to smile and laugh,
Holding a big open heart
in its tanned, work-beaten, hairy chest,
Priceless it is for the modern world,
Very few as there are places such.

64. The Little Sparrow

Passed the long stormy night,
The tiny sparrow saw a world,
Strange and scary enough to turn him
worried for the first time in life.
The sunrays ended the gloom,
Darker was the clouded night,
Light brought but misery more,
Far away was he from his little nest,
'The night storm took away everything,'
Sighed he,
His little body aching due to the strikes
by the unseen drops in the dark,
Aching were the delicate feathers,
due to the buffeting wind,
Shivered the little one,
under the impacts huge.
Remembered he,
how a watery gust
blew away their nest in the dark,
In just one pitiless moment,
lost was the warmth of his siblings,
And gone was parental protection,
Thrown away they were into the night,

as the tree lost its footing.
Played he always there,
Never thought or worried,
Realized he now the opposite,
Piteously ruffled was the fur,
Distorted were feathers,
Desperately he looked for his family
in a nest still intact nearby,
It was a replica of their own world,
Wept the little one with its poor whole,
Thought, he will die.

65. The Shepherd Boy

Lying was he in nature's lap,
While his sheep grazed in
warmth early of a November sun,
Femininely undulating hillside it was,
Rolling pastures,
Overlooking thick-wooded shadowy vales.
The rock beneath gave all he needed:
Felt its hugging warmth and support hard,
Swirling came the breeze by the valley,
Intoxicating it was, as the bright sunrays
stole the bitter pinch.
Shared he the perfect calm,
His herd bleating in harmony,
Rubbing against each other and gambolling,
Running came a little lamb,
Licked his hands,
The master surrendering to the
titillating tinker of love and peace.
Gazed he skywards lazily,
His eyes saturated with nature,
Very thin foamy clouds trailed
across the vast blue unknown,
Same was his existence here.

Faced as he the serenity above,
Forgot the self, shone as his face
under the great fire's light above,
Flew kites tirelessly there,
He too, with imagination unchained.
The wood below across the valley,
Sang with the season;
Some sound broke the silence now and then,
But sweet it was,
As nature was playing with itself.

66. Rain, or Not?

Poor farmers provoked the monsoon,
For it's their last savoir
despite the modernity all,
Farms, cattle, land lifeless feared the burning sand,
Looked meekly for the hope last.
Then came the respite thundering,
Healing them like mother's kiss;
Hayricks, animals, mud-houses,
All made merry with jumpy Utopia,
But to a point only,
Because beyond that misery stares starkly.
Starts the spiritual plight again,
But for the opposite now,
Fee-fawing scarecrow turns the blessing,
As the little life of before,
Gets stalled by the gushing torrents,
Heresy turns all for the low-borns,
It's a world swinging to the extremes,
Never allowing them the stable life of balmy
balance in the middle.
Viciously hammered all with the season—
Paddy appearing just grass over the water sheet,
The cattle gone ownerless,

And the farmers working tirelessly to
drain the great solvent away,
Now they pine for the dry earth;
Dreams of dry, buffeting, blinding sands,
Because water is the foe now.
Zoomed then the drama official,
In all its hypocritical sheen,
Came the dirty hand gloved nicely,
The chameleon offered the rites soft;
Joined mankind nature to plunder emotions.
But the poor people new,
The curse was no irresolvable puzzle,
Hide which can in the nature's maze,
It was simply a man-made flood;
a common way of
saving a great city from getting flooded
by diverting the rich waters
to the poorer fates.

67. Tolerance Divine

Bears society the onslaught,
Abound 'isms' around,
Suppress they the kind, loving natural self,
Dead sea are they,
Drowned is man in,
Modernity aids the evils old,
Making them almost immortal.
Shrinks the world today
with a deadly spasm,
Its small size
not a sign of humanity broad,
But a stone like
exploding dead apathy,
Useless is the human real
for the ultramodern heart,
Centuries tread away,
Tangled is man more;
Inhuman and intolerant manifold.
Yes! The only hope being
the tolerance divine;
The thing humane most,
Able to do good to all.
The chances to survive lie

not so in modernity,
As in being a human real,
Intolerant who is not
like a hardy machine soulless.

68. That Great Flight

Merrily gushed the air,
Happily gyrated the tree compassionate,
Shook the nest; the nestlings became aware
of both good and bad comingled in nature.
Far away were the parents,
Laboriously engaged in ripe corn,
The farmer's little son watched
the birds old, yet littlest to him!
Flew he them away unwillingly,
Due to father's past rebukes,
Subdued which his innocence to give up
fancy and realize the ways of the old.
Flew then the group,
to that dense wood far,
Attracted which always
the little boy's dreamy self.
Flew he also, one day,
On foot to catch his fancy,
Lagged behind but the poor,
for we humans trudge the earth only.
Realized the bird couple,
the plight innocent of the child,
Melt heart theirs for the child,

The same were in the nest.

Flew they slow and halted on the way,

To allow the man's child to catch up,

Joined bird-human to fly,

Delighted which the mother earth.

The boy found himself in a dream;

Stood under the tree,

The birdie kids flapped their wings,

And parentally sang the bird couple.

69. The Weeping 'Dead Place'

Solitary is the place,
Left out almost as a grave,
Comes nobody to live here,
As if a cemetery it is,
Beyond the nature-human tussle of life.
Pulled it never the time's leg,
So passed it swiftly most;
Nothing blossomed here,
Which could drag along,
And force the time to stay and pause.
Shrubs, arid semi,
Rocky foothills small,
Faded grass, poor earth's robe,
Sulks which in clumps,
at places here and there.
Chokes the wind to sing
the prayer for the dead,
Sunrays fall in impassivity,
And wail burningly,
Above is the sky forlorn and discharmed.
Thorny branch sheds tears
motherly for the birds,

But come they not in
the poor mother's clumsy lap;
Play they in gaudy shades elsewhere.
Calls it the humans;
feebly crying to catch someone's attention,
But, unbothered is everyone;
Man as well as nature,
All avoid this place.

70. Zeroed Self for the Crane Couple

The winter is ageing,
The small heaven sulks here,
Wheat's seedlings strong now,
Dew feeds grass healthy,
Meekly await they, only you,
Yes, away you are! But where?
Winter always seemed natural,
Started with your arrival—
Legs long, wings big and beaks strong,
Made you look a bossy bird,
Echoed the horizon with your resounding *cree…k*,
Nothing is same without you.
What is this poor night
without those clarion calls?
Sailed which across the dark,
Now, the same night with
countless twinkling lamps above,
Alas! Missing is its pride.
So dull is the cold rain,
Drops waste without wetting your fur,
Ah, what luck of those
mingled which in your shabby coat!

Now die they in earth,
Tears are they for a chance missed.
Moon cared not about its diminishing size,
As you turned the crescent brighter,
Your gentle movements under
the chilly night played with solitude,
You alone were there to share its sorrow,
Empty now, and suffers alone.
Then, the sun played with earth;
Your shadow proved its essence,
Now, looks it timidly below,
Lost is its identity without you;
Nobody big like you is here
to play with the shining rays.
Red adorned you around the head,
The sky lost its colours in yours bluish gray,
The humans may envy size and
the stormy wind around the wings,
Even other delicate feathers looked strong,
Now, just poor birds are they.
Those long flights brought
the fragrance of land distance,
United was my country,
due to your migrations across it,
We felt unity in diversity,
Landed you down as you here.
Thy long strides measured the land,

Its vastness was proved by you,
Alas, lies it worthless now!
Unfortunate mother, without baby
to measure its maternal depth,
Away are you! Survive or not?
Little was your world,
despite all those bigs about you,
Bird's vapour eyes you were not,
As, lesser was that scary alertness,
And still more, and more, as
I approached you with my humanness.
At a certain night
you tugged at my heart through the ears,
Heart's imagery it was or else,
Maybe just a deep sigh of the past,
I don't know:
At the zero hour
zeroed my imagination and reality.

71. The Human Coronet

So strange are we humans,

Rule a swooning world by faking consciousness,

Take us to be the Kings but slaves we are

to the self-perpetuating mind's yarn,

And always bowed down by the whirling emotions.

A tyrant is this human trait,

But compensates with coronation;

The humans rule with a heavy diadem,

Happy we are to be supreme in the food chain,

But fodder we are to our own selves.

Make we fun of the beasts

for being bald without the coronet;

The crown finds them too low,

So taken they are as light-headed and funny;

And we high with a loaded head.

Lashed is the master by the desires unstoppable,

Cries, wails, neighs, but cannot deny

as a revolting 'no' needs the head's shake,

which the King's craving avoids,

for any browbeat will turn the head bare.

Dressed we are with the shiny fabric

of chronic self-importance,

So much is piled up by the 'thinker'

that it turns a creaky, complaining wagon,
Throw we then our load at others with hate.

72. Nothing Isn't My Village

Testy, desultory or heavenly,

Bright as theism or atheistic blind,

Devoid of twenty-first harum-scarum,

But not a dormouse of the nineteenth,

Nothing is my village, yet all.

Perfect are a few weeks of spring here

even without the famed flowering flora,

The acacia prickles smile

among the lush green branches,

Nature's soldiers last; the green army retreating fast.

Not nature's compassion soft,

Nor concrete's girdle hard,

Soil's warmth scent or burn,

Villagers enjoy the extremes both,

While, the oxen envy the master's stamina.

Law abiding, if they ignore,

Awareness shows only the opposite,

Rises humanity with the sun,

Skilled and unskilled

live here lifefully most.

The summers pass, remain as they

cool to the facilitated islands,

Easily strolls the cold, stay as they warm
to the icy deprivations,
Such are the people here.
Aspire they only a harvest good,
Loss-gain being the sequence,
Teasing nature throws them
on the hard but motherly soil,
Live where they as simple villagers.

73. Little Angels

Little angels, swim in the pond
till the lazy days of late winters,
Flew the elder ducks to reach the hills,
For the nature's law to survive,
Ducklings but too small to fly to the hilly lakes.
Earlier, started the monsoonal song above,
The pond got fed to be a tiny lake,
Secluded and safe turned the adjoining land,
For, no foot treads there
through the chilly winter whole.
And the ducks far in the hills
smell the heaven waiting motherly,
They feel the aroma of peace extreme in the plains,
Despite being so close to the agents of noise,
Arrived they with birdie songs and quacking notes.
Little ones, you were then just hopes,
Eyed the parents the village pond to breed,
Many dreams thronged the waters,
Swam throngs of tiny ducklings among the elders,
Quack-quack started the great birdie game.
Passed the winters; the early born grew,
Many more were the big ducks now,
But alas, the serenity lost,

The silence was conquered,
The spring brought the conquering foot.
Now, your elders sip peace in the hills,
You here; being the last to be born,
Unable to take the flight long,
Pray I, grow thou strong alone!
And conquer the hills with a brave song.

74. Small Farmer

The shifting shades under the sun,
The poor farmer's fate fluctuates with the same,
God watches detached from far,
Test's His creation's performance
through endless nature's play.
A misfit in the modern world,
He desperately tries; turns unfit,
Greater is the loss,
for a misfit can have a hope of salvation,
The unfit loses his rights to dreams all.
Still, the dew shines daughterly,
The morning breeze sooths motherly,
The rising sunrays enhance the small self,
The brave shadow treads bravely afore,
Implores him to be happy and live just for a day.
The birds pass joyfully chirping;
Large becomes the small world,
Walks as he in his little world,
The insects line up to honour,
Confident becomes the poor man.
Fading sounds from the village,
Again remind him of his real worth,
As home is there,

Storehouse of all deprivations and anxiety;
Much to be extracted from the plot small.
Big-hearted he becomes,
Till he reaches the last night's dream,
But alas! Too big for his little parcel of land,
Passes the sweat-drenched day,
only to repeat its old version with the next ray.

75. The Little, Mossy Stepping Stone

I am a round, moss-clad stone

laid as a fording step on this small, shallow riverbed,

I am glistening white on my face,

And moss-skirted around my base,

Sways my stony heart to the gentle tugs

of the shallow, rippling waters,

I, along with my brethren,

Line up to define a path,

across this little pebbled valley,

Humans, you may have a stony heart,

under the soft muscles in your breast,

But mine is definitely

a soft, mellifluous, mossy green one,

And I wear it on my sleeve,

While you step over my clean white face,

And scamper away,

I just pray,

Safe you reach,

Without any further breach.

76. Mossy Fluidity

In the mossy fluidity of a solitary pool
in a lonely vale,
An open, welcoming canvas,--
Mossy green, pale yellow, rusted brown and mottled gray,
As a tired traveller I stand and
see my shadows while the mountain breeze hail,
My spread self mixed with the mossy waters,
And I marvel at the small canvas holding the image,
While the brook tries to rewrite the colours.

77. God! Who or What are You?

God, reside thou where?

In a simpleton's easy, empty mind,

or an intellectual's heavy, shiny brain?

Fill you an innocent, almost empty child,

or burst from the laden, wise old?

Sun's warm rays are you

that bathes us with life?

Or the dark, blind night,

imitate when we death and forgetfulness?

God, which facet of appearance you are?

The winner's pride are thou?

Or sulk through the defeated?

The water around a lotus

or the parched land below thorns?

God, which extreme you are?

Ever blooming, fade not,

or rejuvenate now and then?

Punishment to the guilty

or mother's soft hand to the wronged,

God, what art thou?

Strong's heavy impact are you,

or the weak's escape?

Whether the animals in the jungle,
or most social are you?
God, which thing art you?
Humane more than humanity,
or a taboo you are to avoid?
Whose master are you?
Of those devouts in temples and shrines,
or just a common good being?

78. The Wind from Dreamland

O wind, come you from far,
From that land beyond dreams,
which the eyes never saw, nor ears heard,
and the sleep missed even in dreams;
Bless thou! You enable my senses
to feel, hear, see and dream.
I dream with eyes open,
Of the land distant,
Thy touch makes me
imagine all that must be
now happening there,
Circle as you around me.
Those small hills rounded,
With pastures, scattered trees,
Clouds playing with the sun,
And the laughing blue also,
The distant howl of a wolf,
and the bleating lambs straighten their ears.
I accompany that tiller
walking barefoot, on the way
to his small farm and
touch the tools he shoulders,

And wish him the best of potatoes,
O air, I can feel his worries also.
I look at that house far away,
On that flat ledge by the hillside,
Chimney smokes, doors closed,
Family gathered around a table,
And listen to their chit-chat,
O wind, I can see their balmy routine.
My heart feels their feelings,
They worry about the father
gone to the nearest town;
One of them going to the window
and stare into the misty distances
of the winding, hilly path.
I walk on the grass unbeaten,
which softly pricks with virginal blades,
Nobody must have walked here
except some lone animal,
Or, some forlorn love-drenched soul,
I rest on the green carpet now and close my eyes.
Sit now under a luxuriant tree's canopy,
Few must have rested here,
A bird chirps above in the green,
Heart beats with its melody,
And the notes go spreading
and surrendering to the majestic solitude.
There flows a brook,

Its gentle murmur on the pebbled bed,
The eyes see a fluid canvas:
Sand, pebbles and fishes,
I now dip my legs in the water,
I feel rain somewhere up.
O wind, I can live all that scene,
Distances have melted,
You mixed that hilly essence
as you swept over the charming panorama,
That is the world only for me,
As nobody else hears, sees or dreams it.

79. Betrayed Self of the Indian Soul

Runs today this country, but how?
Gazing up to its stars, who
sowed the potential seeds of mass destiny,
Oof, defeated now by its masses own!
Their self vouched for a nation great,
But now self-betrayed most,
Self-defeating today's youth
listen not the soulful cries of those martyred.
Ripe fruits they were,
Thrust themselves in freedom's crusher,
Blood came pure, while the fleshy mass
and powdered bones smiled in the dust.
Those dying heaps of flesh dreamt
a rainbow-hued nation,
Alas, we stomped over their blood's carpet,
With monstrous hoofs of every sort.
Torn out dream it's now, smiling in some old eye,
While we run hoarsely, sometimes just to
pick up certain dusted piece
on some anniversary or the other.
Nehru's 'productive hands' throttle others;
Non-violence simply an impractical antonym,

This nation will wither; its rulers show
moral corruptibility extreme; subjects do the same.
Gasps this nation for life, its body
sixty years old, clad in wornouts,
Holding its staggering and crawling billion souls,
But for how long, I am afraid to guess!

80. Mother

So many things exist, to whom
one must shed the pungent sense of self,
But the murky self always neighs,
Making a nimble, smart, selfish, social dummy.
Stretch such things till the stars,
Whom our desires turn to dust around our feet,
Although measurable not,
Mother is but the loser most.
Machine is this society,
Operates on input-output principle,
Vary the losses among different relations,
Ever-giving mother is but the giver biggest.
All her relations take it through:
Parents as the 'other's property',
Outshines husband as the hope last,
And children fatten on her maternity.
Mother of pearl she is,
Harder the shell, the better it is,
One day, sulks which empty, the pearl gone,
Suffers she with the hollow title of an ideal mother.
Most imbalanced is her equation,
Fattest is the oaf on the opposite;
Melts her in childhood,

And befools in his youth.
Mowed down in the old age,
Obsolete and ignored manifold,
Dies she before herself,
Without any solace even from the past.

81. The Orthodox Proverb

Work hard, you will get a reward—
It's drilled deep in childhood soft,
A saying it's only then,
Simple minds find it the elders' trick,
Who any way must find fault
and ordain so many things unplayful.
The same proverb spreads its tentacles,
Grows it with the body,
Burden it is not now,
But a necessity to survive,
And they obey its command,
What a devil! Free by now.
The adults are serious enough
about name, fame and glory,
Dedicate they themselves to a cause,
Create a glass palace so huge,
Crumbles which one day,
Splintered pieces cut through the flesh.
The evil survives still,
Now through the sympathetic pout,
Except the sulking self, the universe parrots it,
What can the poor soul do?
If not aspire for the palace again,

Alas, the fate repeats itself most often!
Success is rarely the outcome,
If it comes, greater is the endeavour,
somehow doomed to fail another time,
And if not, failure is loosened
from the garb it had taken,
Both lead to the same age-old futility.
Battered is failure through pompous words,
To get ready the wounded,
And obey the immortal proverb's command,
Dies it never, only we perish,
Even the dying is wished to
succeed in the life next!
There is no other way,
But to fall in its trap,
It's supposed to last
even after the death,
If the saying has an exception,
Then please, tell me one!

82. The Lost Light

Stumbled I across
the rugged mountain track,
Tall pines lingered above,
The gigantic peaks snubbed,
I felt the smallest there.
Cold air touched peaks,
Higher they appeared still,
Shrivelled I and crinkled,
Passed clouds above swiftly,
Confirmed piteous lowness mine.
Trifling I felt,
Took them as ghosts around,
Subdued I was,
Less by the body weak,
But more in the mind.
My eyes saw piteously,
Sick was my soul
in getting fooled by the pessimistic eyes,
Aching were my legs,
More by the weakness imagined.
Earlier, the sun illuminated
the whole valley alongside,
Living were all except me,

Now, setting it was,
And imminent was gloom.
Knew I, the lost opportunity,
Wasted I the entire day
in seeing desperate dark,
Now, manifold it was,
Realized I, the lost light.

83. The Eulogy, Vanished

Frowned upon he was,
As failed he all expectations,
Own was fault,
Lived he on others' dreams.
Like a slave he was,
Wasted life whole;
Did as the master wanted,
Died then empty all.
Always he cried hoarsely,
Sand song theirs,
Bleeding were his own
deep inside the imprisoned self.
Eulogized he was then,
Renowned became the grave,
Rot inside which the flesh
of the dead heart's unsung song.
Fame he took it to
crush his own heart's freedom,
Played they with it,
While his soul cried.
Expected they still more
from the slavish being,
Crumpled which under the demand,

A living grave he turned.
Now uncouth history he was,
Same was the grave,
Alas, eulogy had vanished
like his powdered bones in the grave.

84. Last Death

Dirty song is life, peeled off
throats of those who sing this grisly verse,
It is a curse,
we get it due to past births' misdeeds.
Why was I born? Only to
continue breathing like a statue,
every cycle pinches; why all
live to be murdered at each step?
I aspire to live, but always
lynched to death, which comes never,
Leaves me tossing and bleeding,
I pray for the divine death only.
Skinny dog paddling for life,
With a mute look in the waters dangerous,
Alas, destined to be drowned!
A bird with chipped wings I am.
So much takes out every breath,
Appears this nature feeding on me—
The soul escapes nostrils every second,
I hate all, drink they my soul's blood.
Cursed never to act or imagine,
As these always fall on me;
Strike like a thunderbolt,

And there I lay tossing in pain.
The time will come when I will
become passive to the hunter's arrows,
Nothing will remain to make Him happy;
Die when will I for the last time.
Alas, it's a dream, not to be true,
I know, I won't meet the death last,
as long as I wish for it,
As I'm destined to fail even in this wish.

85. Falling in a Pit

Too far and deep

I have gone into the pit of gloom,

And lost in the cavernous folds

of the impending doom,

Even the brightest big suns

now appear too far and take puns,

Faint stars these now

and just flash their inspiring rays,

Feeble rays reaching me cannot take out

the ship caught in treacherous bays,

I know the futility of the beckoning light,

Even in its brightest folds outside,

hope was always out of sight,

Now I go deep into my night,

With nobody as a witness to my plight,

All cherished dreams out of sight,

A wingless bird that tried to fly

but then crashed from its struggled height,

Now I just silently walk into

the dark hold of my night,

Alone

and forlorn,

The musicality of my soft moan,

Carrying me into hitherto unreachable zone.

86. One Special Speciality

Thou are all speciality;
Standing above the ordinary,
You pleasantly cuddle my psyche,
Everlasting is the image,
Such is rarity yours.
Eureka! Ethereal evasiveness yours,
Exalted is the examinee,
As the human self aspires always
exemption from the commonness around,
Thou make me feel special.
Speciality, fragrance distinct,
Aspire which humans all;
Asphodel singled out in orchard,
Smiles which like the rarest blossom,
And I become privileged more.
Emotions about you perfect me,
Assuage the beast inside,
Attar sweetest you are,
By which austere is not
the world abounding in trivialities.
Need humans an aurora new,
Subdued in the race mad,
I like you as an axiom of beauty,

But not just for my sake,
Rather for the humanity whole.
All should aspire for
one lyrical lyre special,
Last hope it is for
the defeating self in a world ghoulish,
Salvager, aspire I always thou.

87. The Dying Day, Unwanted

Day! You now prepare to go,
Exactly one thousand years ago
brother your did the same,
Repeat thou now history,
For man's sake, the millennium new!
The ageing process of humanity—
The new millennium,
New hopes and aspirations,
Grew we up by a thousand years,
Thus historically old,
Pretend now to be kids,
And get jumpy-grumpy in pell-mell celebrations.
You, who will carry the billions
laden on your chariot,
While they will rejoice,
Unmindful of the old, greying carrier.
You, ready to die a universal death
without ageing anyone,
As they pluck off you from
the reach of the biological clock,
Or infinite pendulum's swing,
Billions of aspirations and load,

Like ant swarms,
they queue up to the holes next—
The looming unknown and dark millennium,
And you who proudly hold
the baton for the last time,
Stand here alone,
watching the mob trudging forward,
You, who like thousand brothers yours
bore the brunt of thousand years' flurry,
Obeyed the command of God—
'Falter never or choke!
Let them go!'

88. Let the Change Prevail Inside

This chilly gentle breeze of a defined era
blankets us for the last,
This sun struggling in the fog,
Tries to see us for the last.
From a long slumber we arise,
On this millennium's last dawn,
The moon in its last phase
still gracing the western sky,
And through its bloated,
Obscured shape in the west,
Stubbornly watches the hoopla,
The millennium eve's noise.
God! Amidst such fire-cracking 'lasts',
About the matter and externalities,
Will the 'lasts' extend
to the dark corners in us?
The patches where
greed, selfishness, war
and all man-made disasters
vying with the nature's,
Will they also pack off
to follow the trend around.

O night, when you arrive today,
Please chuck away all the dirt
in thy nocturnal folds:
O sun, cast your ochre rays
oblique upon the wrong facets,
Make them glow like jewels;
O breeze, enter the souls,
Soothe the passion inside,
Blow up which like volcano;
O man, let the series culminating around,
enter your deeper self and make you realise,
the futility of sticking to old follies
even in the new era.

89. The Millennium Bath

A bath I am to have today,
The 'after death' ritual
for the mortals left behind;
The old millennium will die today.
The certainty of its death,
And the certainty of timing as well!
I want to be certain myself;
Wash I will, the mortal remains.
The remains of the millennium last,
Quantified efforts to measure eternity,
A part of me will also die today,
Fragmented death to live fully another day.
Die with the millennium,
A thousand years old man,
Wash I will myself,
Midnight is the hour to depart.
We will go hand in hand,
The remains will be left behind—
All washed out and infants;
Millennium new, and the new man.
That is why I will bathe
for the new man, millennium new,
We know, the new may loath the old;

Two thousand-year-olds.
Try I will to oblate the sins,
And all the sewage and garbage,
Layered which over both of us,
I will bathe for both today.

90. Some Celebrating Lamps

Celebrations will occur today,
With firecrackers and partying
on happy islands on the west coast,
Noise huge, colours bright
will try to subdue something.
Something which plagues the east,
The hush and fury in the dark,
Arrowed upon poorly quantified humanity,
Died where even the little traces of quality and dignity,
And celebrations will take place in the west.
Those drunken dances and rockets flying,
The rich garbage of celebration scattered around,
Myriads swaying upon the boozed beaches,
With joy, sensuousness and laughter,
While deadly claws put a print on the sand in the east.
The east spread out like an orphan,
The forlorn beaches, where swept out
were the labouring footprints of masses,
The night where howls around
the decaying uncremated remains.
And unmindful and uncaring
they will celebrate the night whole,

For new dawn, millennium new,
Hope has died meanwhile
somewhere with the millennium gone.
Such is the case with humans,
Segmented society for roles,
The lucky ones with a lamp
to welcome the change great,
Others carried on bier in the dark.

91. There is Always Light Somehow

There is light beyond
the deepest dark depth,
There is a bright day after
the ghostly haunts of a nightmarish night,
After a barren famished fight
there is a full blossomed spring's delight,
After pining pangs of separation
there is a worthy end to the desperation,
After crashing in the gutters
there is a surge and rise to bathe in holy waters,
After crying convulsions on the lips,
a smile takes honeyed sips,
After the last defeat,
still there is an undying urge to accomplish the feat,
Even when blind with despair,
there is hope hiding and cajoling somewhere,
Even in hate love still lurks somewhere!

92. The Millennium takes a Big Toll

The millennium is to end,

So will be the case with the century,

Approaches as this day the zero hour;

Aah, this narrowing down,

Too eager to embrace the next,

The altar of nationalism too

looks for some selfless sacrifice,

The stale flowers of its glorious past,

Now need some offerings fresh.

On this 31st of December,

alarmed is this mortal

for the countdown quickened,

The relatives few weep hoarsely,

For their loved ones,

Hijacked at a land distant;

Nationalism is thirsty,

It demands sacrifice,

A billion souls expecting a few hundred people

to assuage their boiling sense of nationhood,

But the pain of one's own blood

is felt only by the closest kin.

Their pointing fingers,

And slogans for the release
of someone who challenged
our integrity, our pride,
They have to put self above the nation,
Jingoism is on a hypothetical plane,
The realty cuts us to our real size.
Wails, cries and noises,
Chorused a pleading, 'Release',
For a week whole,
Nationalism squirmed meanwhile,
Dreams of national glory postponed
to save the blood in real life,
Struck was a bargain
to save those who constitute the nation.
Three militants go free,
Hundreds died to capture whom,
Our soldiers look mute,
Bullets in their chests
though pain not much,
But then there are tears of joy
as the captives walk free,
Nationalism may feel the pinch,
But is it above the life of its ordinary citizens?
This millennium can seek comfort,
As another will follow figuratively,
Nationalism but must be feeling
a fishy death out of the pond,

Suffocated to death;
Vanish as the oxygen from the lungs,
The hawks may condemn them as selfish,
But is it a sin to cry to save one's kin?
Earlier, some soldiers kidnapped for
the cause same were slaughtered,
Nobody then barked 'Release',
O my God,
A soldier taken guaranteed to die.
The hostages will return tonight,
Under pressure by the citizens,
The painful wails shut out
all nationalistic doors in the state,
And they will celebrate,
Some 160 families will rejoice extra,
But they should light candles also
for those who died in Kargil,
Everybody jingled when
with pride and love for the nation,
Certain as they were of safety,
Died meanwhile our soldiers icy deaths.
Yes, we will celebrate today
the approach of the millennium new;
And the great guffaws will echo around,
Hysterically rising towards
the zero hour approaching,
But at what cost?

A question difficult to answer.

93. My Sleepy Village on the Millennium Eve

The new millennium will

take birth in a couple of hours

in the foggy dark with the stars blown out.

What kind of handover is this?

When we see no light,

Either in the houses or starry twinklings above.

The dusk today was prematurely lost in fog,

Not a single star smiled,

Starless, light-less we go into the changeover.

Same in the houses, blackouted,

We here in this sleepy village

lie abed in the archaic dark.

Surely the fog will last

for another half of the day to come,

Sunless, we will welcome the newborn triplets.

Millennium, century, day;

The momentous birth-time in the dark,

Electric bulbs in houses also follow nature in gloom.

Of course, luminosity is there somewhere,

At places some; houses privileged,

Bulbs glow, create as they stars new.

Lucky they are,

Take part in the natal activities,
And the partisan, crony-crazed new one arrives.
And we the irritating ones,
Shunned for not taking part in the celebrations
at the long anticipated moment of break in history.
Uncertain we are thus,
What change has for us?
The stale old dry dust or some fresh dew?
The night is thus cold and dark,
Great events will occur,
Our fate but hardly provides any succour.

94. The Night in Labour Pain

The night is in labour pain today,

I can feel its sweat, suffering and plight.

Triplets are to be born today—

The millennium, the century, the day.

Labour pain is too much—

Wars, epidemics, killings kicked her belly.

For years one thousand she bore

the pregnancy period all turbulent and disturbed.

The pain is thus too much,

Yet birth she has to give for new life.

A new child among the maternal pains,

The elder one meanwhile writhing to die.

And look at the urgency,

Sky has touched the ground almost.

A smoky fog circles around

to work as a midwife.

Too many kicks have been hurled at the belly,

Pain hence cannot be avoided.

Painful writhing more so,

For the birth time's certainty is there.

Also scared is the mother

of those rioters awaiting the birth.

God forbid, if they go crazy,
and kick at the moment last.
Anxious for the infant,
She fears pangs more.
Small hope is there in a lamp
glowing dimly by death bed.
But a furious whiff by anyone
can blow it out too.

95. Midnight Crowning

Now that clock has struck twelve,
We have entered the millennium new;
The grand ceremonial crowning,
Celebrations for which were going on
among hopes, fears, opportunities new.
The court members are jubilant,
Exult at this moment,
The rest, meanwhile, remain unconscious,
Even about the newly crowned!
What type of coronation is this?
That people nearest to the ground understand it not,
Just a time-pass game perhaps,
Still, on this foggy cold night,
When voices are heard high and near,
Thanks to the dense foggy medium,
The noise made here or there
travels disproportionate to the source's distance,
And the majority just takes a turn,
Lying while in their beds.
Isn't it an unsuitable time?
For they must sleep now,
While the crowning ceremony
being held at this freezing zero hour,

When few must be awake
and left with celebrity nocturnal spirit,
Sleep they will like bats and owls
when the day will break,
And the rest will start toiling,
Unmindful of the nocturnalities.
Of course, new sun, new day
will be there for them,
Its meaning but will be unnoticeable;
Hungry, deprived bellies never
sense theoretical change in the cosmos as such.

96. Three Big Zeroes for All

At this zero hour I stand in the dark,
trying to see the newcomer,
Nobody is there, alas!
Not even the refracted skylight.
Bundled out round in a circle,
I thus fumble around words,
Meaning whose has fatality—
Of circling around; ending nowhere.
Three big zeroes of the new,
which hover over, gobble up
the sleepy environment around me,
Wonder while I about the 'zeroness'.
Three zeroes take me round—
The zero for myself,
A bigger one for the country,
Still larger one for the world whole.
Will I break this vicious circle
of rounding on the path same;
Burning out too much energy,
Arriving then at nothing?
Will this country having
so many self-centred circles,

Arrive at something new,
rather than the same big zero?
And what about this world?
Will it unmatch its physical shape?
The great big circle,
Binds which our orbiting passions.

97. Of New Glimpses, New Rays

The new sun, millennium new,
Rays new at Dong, Katchel,
Pray I, crown my India anew!
New with a newly hewed crown
with hopes of more survival,
Not so with basics, rather
new roles, responsibilities new.
That India which saw
so much of flux and turbulence
over thy last empire—
History of religions,
Of races, ideas and many more,
Pray I, the newly diademed
remain such in the millennium next.
O new sun, shine too bright,
To light the patches dark,
Haunt which the geography ours,
And shadows whose reach hearts,
Sun, please warm up our hearts
with new warm ideas,
Glow with such spiritual aura
that the highest peaks in the Himalayas

shine like a jewel on the head,
O light, traverse through body
'Hindustan' to most distant parts;
Each hut, each palace, each home,
Light them, do away with the dark.
God, we committed wrongs,
Blood spilled over,
Minds became rigid; misunderstood,
Pray I, o new rays,
Warm up them again,
Blanket up the wrong,
O new sun,
Shine with vibrancy such.

98. New Dawn—Warm Rays for Frigid Fate

The days are in fact trotting,
A new dawn, new year, of course
new century and millennium,
The snaily destiny but pulls back.
Time may fly past,
Making us grow manifold,
We but remain stony,
rigid and preyed upon by chance.
Moves it too slowly,
Whom spirit never catches,
Its rock-like firmness,
makes us stick mossily around.
I do not know
what the new rays have in store?
Better or worse?
Rays to see or to blind?
Today I start my new day;
A new start and initiative,
Let me see if the occasion special
lends its hues to me also.
My palette has just two colours,
Just black and white,

Let me see if it gets multi-coloured,
Giving me a new rainbow.
I do not know whether the new dawn
is a different one, after the night long,
When darkness grappled with me and I failed,
Or is it the same as the old?
Let me see the occasion
too special and celebrity,
Prismatic and multicoloured,
Too long was the one-coloured night.
O new rays,
Please turn the occasion special,
God please, leave I myself
at thy complete mercy.

99. The Midnight's Throaty Call

The great call at midnight:
'Will the throaty pitch and guffaw
be the same for the thousand years coming?'
If it's to be such,
Please, then let us all
turn to nothingness at this moment.
Nothing new does it seem:
The chorus behind the throaty
noise seems to be the same foolish dream.
Such a huge and godly definition
given to the change,
Most forgettable is which,
but parroted now with childish rage.
Godliness has been contrived out of it,
I'm afraid it will bear the end same;
Revered now most formally,
Misunderstood and negated afterwards,
In all practices which
the sun will uncover at the dawn.

100. A Cosily Safe Smile Somewhere

The spring's traces last,
Hot summers approaching fast,
Languid notes in the air,
A solitary bird's forlorn chirping
for its musical share,
Drowned in stillness
this late morning bright and fair,
The sky's dull blue,
Spread with some mystical clue,
But a smaller world is there,
The overall unease cannot reach where,--
In its self-defined world
in a corner tiny,
The luscious wild flower
still stands brave and shiny.

101. Indefatigable Beauty

The storm screeched through the night,
Poured its fury through sadistic love-bite,
Undefeated but smiles the beauty,
Still doing its fragrant duty,
Her holy petals bear
the storm's violating drops without fear,
Holy beads now they are,
Smiles, smiles and no war!

102. Little Master Corona

O thou little master,
The world was a bit faster,
You now force brakes,
Lions turn into drakes,
Even newspaper is scary,
No longer a news-carrying fairy,
It comes from Delhi,
Fear pinches my guts and belly,
With inhibitions I touch,
A fearful world is such.

103. The Story of a Frost-beaten Tree

The winter has been brutal and harsh,
And my struggle turned almost a farce,
Lost all my leaves,
With loss my soul grieves,
Still not all is lost,
For greenish life finds a host
in the wheat at my feet,
They pay a respectable greet,
My loss and my pain
don't go in vain,
Tumbled down as my leaf
with pain and grief,
Blossom thousands around,
Wheatlings like daughters doth surround,
Fell where my tear,
Many a smile this earth doth bear,
Doesn't go waste my pain,
Sows it the prospects of gain,
If not for me,
Definitely for thee.

104. The Light

The light does hark,
beyond the deepest dark,
There is a day bright,
after the ghostly haunts of a nightmarish night,
After a barren famished fight,
there blossoms the spring's delight,
After pining pangs of separation,
there is a worthy end to the desperation,
After crashing in the gutters,
there is a surge and rise to bathe in holy waters,
After crying convulsions on the lips,
a smile takes honeyed sips,
After the last defeat,
still there is an undying urge to accomplish the feat,
Even when blind with despair,
there is hope hiding and cajoling somewhere,
Even in hate, love still lurks somewhere.

105. Lost

It has been months since
I last lit my faith's lamp,
So many days have passed since
prayers chimed in my dark den's air damp,
My meditating self,
Now gives atheistic yelp.
Lost my faith!
Lost my prayer!
Lost my rituals!
Lost my meditative trance!

106. A Story

The story told by the soul to its own corpse:
Once I flew and frolicked high,
Now the flesh and blood gone dry,
The real me withdrew with a painful sigh,
They say, 'I was destined to die,'
It's but the biggest lie!

107. The Night

Too far and deep,

I have gone into the pit of gloom,

And lost in the cavernous folds

of the impending doom,

Even the brightest big suns

now appear too far,

Faint stars these now

that just flash their feebly inspiring rays,

The feeble raylets reaching me

cannot take out the ship caught in treacherous bays,

I know the futility of the beckoning light,

Even in its brightest folds outside,

hope was always out of sight,

Now I go deep into my night,

With nobody as a witness to my plight,

All cherished dreams out of sight,

A wingless bird that tried to fly

but then crashed from its struggled height,

Now I just silently walk

into the dark hold of my night,

Alone

and forlorn,

The echo of my soft moan,

carrying me into hitherto unreachable zone.

108. Holy Fire

I am the moth
and I love my flame!
My fire!
But I feel the burning core of
the glow around which
I helplessly circle around!
I know that I cannot stop
the fire from burning,
So I throw myself in a fiery pit
to forget my dear flame's burning plight!
I throw myself in a bigger fire
so that I forget myself
and my flame's cries!

109. Midnight Musings

A few night-blossoming jasmine flowers muse:
Dewy fun under nightly sun
Swathed in the cool shades of a dewy night,
We stand brave with smiles and innocent delight,
When all sleep,
we hold the beacon of love and light,
The moon is our sun,
When you will get up in the morning,
you can't imagine how much was the nightly fun!

110. Sweet Pangs of Nostalgia

Holding a dream in my fist,

Staring at the misty past

and forcing myself not to see the future

eager to unfold itself too fast,

I wave at the nostalgic strains

still beckoning and faintly alive,

How I wish I could dive

back into the pools of the past,

To have my moments last

at a place that held me in its cradle soft,

That pious embrace which still holds me aloft!

111. A Fatherly Whisper

Parental love loops around with a new ray
on an early winter day,
The mighty lord whispers in a soft voice,
'My son grow thou strongest in spirit
and sire chances for those without any choice!'